PEACE *by the* SEA

PEACE *by the* SEA

Inspiring Images and Quotes to Light Your Way

DIANE....

FIND PEACE BY THE SEA

HARRY L. THOMAS, MSW

EDITED BY LAURIE HEYDEN, MS

Mountain Arbor Press

Alpharetta, GA

ISBN: 978-1-63183-980-1 - Paperback

Printed in the United States of America 1 2 0 7 2 0

∞ This paper meets the requirements of ANSI/NISO Z39.48-1992 (Permanence of Paper)

Cover design by Kelly Coccio
Cover photo by Harry L. Thomas

This book is dedicated to my mom and dad,
Mildred Thomas and Clem Thomas Jr.
Thank you for showing me how to live a
purposeful and fulfilling life.

The ocean stirs the heart,
inspires the imagination,
and brings eternal joy to the soul.

—Robert Wyland

Contents

Acknowledgments

The ocean, after all, is not about stability,
but about change. Change is normal.
Everything changes. All the time.

—Wendy Williams

I want to acknowledge Wendy Williams for being influential in sparking my career as a writer and producer, and teaching me that no goal is out of reach.

I acknowledge Eugene Cobb, my first photography instructor, who instilled in me the importance of capturing on film a moment in time.

I would like to thank the following people for the various ways they have supported my emotional, physical, spiritual, and professional well-being:

George Allard
Alec Asten
Chris Bahn
Richard Bennett
Geoff Blanchette
Naomi Calhoun
John Carboni
Kelly Coccio
Sandra D. Coleman
Billy Cote
Kris Cote Jr.
Dr. Umer Darr
Dr. Martin Hellman
Laurie Heyden
Arshenna Hines
Chris James
Gilda James
Rose Jones
Ryan Kristafer
Wally Lamb
Uzi Mann
Pat Marshall
Stephen Martin
Tommy McKissick
Mike McLaughlin
Ann Moore
Shane Moore
Mike Morissette
Maria O'Connor
Dr. Richard Peng
Jim Pitka
Dave Plowden
Rita Powers, CSA
Maria L. Ramos
Nazim Salihu
Atty. Scott Sawyer
Rollin Sealey
Jim Spinnato
Joan Zubres-McIntyre-Sullivan
Robin Turner
Ben Ward
Tracy Wilder
Phil Yanaway

I am deeply grateful to the following writers, celebrities, and leaders, whose quotes have inspired inner strength in me:

Lailah Gifty Akita
Israelmore Ayivor
T. A. Barron
Dave Barry
Alexander Graham Bell
Roy T. Bennett

Hassan Blasim
Bodhidharma
Cory Booker
Kobe Bryant
Warren Buffett
Nicholas Murray Butler
Eddie Cantor
Shrestha Das Choudhury
Adrienne Clarkson
Paulo Coelho
William "Bootsy" Collins
Nick Cummins
Antoine de Saint-Exupéry
Matshona Dhliwayo
Drake
Dr. Wayne Dyer
Roger Ebert
Max Ehrmann
Empire
Tim Fargo
Devika Fernando
Robert Fulghum
Mahatma Gandhi
Steve Gilliland
Sandy Gingras
Sydney J. Harris
Lauryn Hill

Conrad Hilton
Anthony T. Hincks
Holstee, Inc.
Langston Hughes
Idillionaire
Mehmet Murat İldan
Lady Bird Johnson
Roxana Jones
Harley King
Martin Luther King Jr.
Jana Kingsford
Jarod Kintz
Miss Kitty
Lorde
Sophia Loren
Juri Love
Martian Manhunter
Bryant McGill
A. A. Milne
Thomas S. Monson
Montague Workshop
Van Morrison
Steven Morrissey
Debasish Mridha
Malcolm Muggeridge
Max Müller
Friedrich Nietzsche

Nemo Nox
Barack Obama
Andrew O'Hagan
Erika Oppenheimer
Brad Paisley
Carl Perkins
Pablo Picasso
Ken Poirot
Jane Poynter
Rumi
David Russell
Louis Sachar
Carlos Santana
Ruta Sepetys
Dr. Seuss
Robin Sharma
Brooke Shields
Sir Philip Sidney
Pastor Sean Smith
Alysha Speer
Dr. Stephen Strange
Charles R. Swindoll
Emilia Wickstead
Wendy Williams
Oprah Winfrey
Zhuangzi
Zig Ziglar

Foreword

Peace. It is a state of being that often eludes us in modern times. Harry L. Thomas was onto something when he fell into his daily peace ritual. For years, this multitalented entrepreneur and former professor of social work has relied upon a daily practice of choosing a motivating quote and spending time by the sea to self-reflect. This personal routine has helped him to find balance, cope with stress, and focus on personal goals.

Peace by the Sea is a compilation of Harry's combinations of photos and quotes, organized by a key set of principles for how to live your best life. Harry's principles are relevant to all and promote resilience, a healthy attitude, strong coping skills, and inner strength. Harry illustrates his principles with his personal seaside photography, which he carefully pairs with uplifting quotes. The quotes inspire introspection, self-reflection, and personal growth.

This timely book offers hope and personal guidance at a challenging time in history. Harry's chapters shine light during dark times on a pathway to self-care. Due to the stressful challenges of life, it is important to engage in self-care to build a stronger, more compassionate self. We all need to be restored to a greater state of emotional health after dealing with stress. Self-care is a key coping strategy for personal well-being.

The sea is the perfect venue to find personal renewal. Peaceful images of the sea make it easier to think clearly, let go of frustration, and find inner strength. By self-reflecting, we dig deeper to find renewed fortitude. Self-reflection fine-tunes the quality of our choices. Strength comes from character. Self-reflection is the route to character.

Step into each photograph. Savor the seaside experience each photograph brings to mind. Process each quote as it applies to your life. Take your time and self-reflect. Self-reflection brings you one step closer to living your best life.

—Laurie Heyden, MS

School Psychologist

What Is the Magic of the Sea?

Laurie Heyden, MS

What is this magic the sea possesses, this power to bring peace?

Is it magical, or is it science? How is it that we so easily find comfort by the shoreline? Is it the fresh, oxygen-rich air? Could it be the scent of the ocean, hearkening back to pleasant childhood memories? Is there some health benefit of the salty air that our lungs can't get enough of? Is it the sound of wind and water, a rhythmic white noise that somehow soothes the soul? Is it the clarity of thought that happens in the open space by the sea? Is it the majesty of the ocean making us feel small yet interconnected with the rest of the universe? Is it the fresh outlook that readily sets in as our problems shrink in magnitude against an infinite backdrop of bountiful blueness? Is it the water itself that brings a sense of revival—for the weary crave the trusted promise of leisure graciously fulfilled by beaches, rivers, and lakes alike? How is it that we often leave such oases feeling grounded, strengthened, and restored? Is it the change of scenery—an overdue break from reality? Is that the magic of the sea?

Is the gift of peace found in the perpetual and comforting rhythms of nature? Is it the push and pull of the elements that tip us back perfectly into balance? As sure as the waves rush away, they glide right back to tag the sand. Is it the flirtatious invitation to play like a child again? Is the ebb and flow of the waves a clue that we should seek balance? Is peace found in a gentle balance between give and take, service and self-care? Does instinct drive us to breathe in mirrored unison with the mighty Atlantic, inhaling peace, exhaling anxiety, letting go of frustration and disappointment? Does the sea have a resetting effect on our biorhythms, grounding us deeply to the heartbeat of the Earth? Is it the graceful rise and fall of the tides—a gentle sway with the moon? Is it the comfort of a rising tide reaching out to befriend a lonely moon?

Are we humbled by the synchronous movement of water on the

Earth's surface, a tango between distant continents as she turns reliably on a delicate axis, the great marker of time? As sure as the sun sets over the blue horizon, it can be trusted to rise again. Is it the hope of a new dawn over cool waters, the faithful promise of a new tomorrow?

Is it the multisensory experience of sight, sound, smell, and feel of the gentle wind that restores our soul? Perhaps it is all of this. We don't know exactly why the sea brings us peace, but it does, and it keeps us coming back. A seaside visit satiates the senses, distracting us from the grind of daily life. The seaside is a refuge from the trivialities and burdens we endure. The power of the sea is to ground the spirit in a healthy perspective and open a fresh space in our mind for new ideas and better possibilities. It is the perfect place to self-reflect and see creative solutions to that which burdens us.

The peace we find by the sea is a reliable source of hope that rarely disappoints. A message echoes in the wind: Relax. Reflect. Restore. Renew. Realize that all will be well. Embrace the possibility that you can live your best life.

Introduction

There are two things that give me peace of mind and clarity: a good picture and a great quote. This book is a compilation of wisdom, guidance, and imagery to inspire personal strength and inner peace. It reflects my personal formula for living my best life.

Inspiring words resound in my mind as I chart my course through life. I was raised in a household where life's lessons were taught in short, meaningful quotes. My mother, Mildred Thomas, being a "master of quotes," would often speak her own eloquent nuggets of wisdom or reference the words of world leaders and philosophers who inspired her. As an adult, I started quoting her and actively applying her words of wisdom to my personal life. "As my mother used to say" is a phrase that has preceded many of my daily statements in conversation with others.

I continue to rely on inspirational quotes to illuminate how I can live my best life. As I have evolved through my life experiences, I have developed a daily ritual of finding meaningful quotes to motivate me and light my way. Succinct gems of wisdom have guided my decisions and choices in my personal life.

Living by the sea has really enriched my life. I've felt privileged to live my whole life by the water, enjoying the therapeutic sense of well-being it provides. The power of the blue sea and mighty ocean to bring inner peace, clarity of thought, and a sense of freedom is undeniable. I continue to make daily trips to the ocean to reflect on my life and restore a sense of peace to my soul.

During my formative years, I developed a love for photography. Since then, I have always had my camera close by to capture those spontaneous picture-perfect moments in nature. In recent years, I have maintained a self-development ritual of picking out an uplifting quote each day to match one of my favorite shots. The quotes are carefully selected to sustain my emotional and spiritual well-being. Keeping my mind, body, and soul healthy has helped me to achieve my daily goals as an actor, writer, and producer.

Throughout my life, I've narrowed down key guiding principles as a foundation for living my best life. I choose to live by these and consider them in making my daily choices. These include having a humble perspective, being grateful, seizing my own personal power, acknowledging emotions, being authentic, stepping out of my comfort zone, finding direction and purpose, having a strong work ethic, overcoming obstacles, making tough decisions, nurturing social connections, unlocking the heart, and achieving piece within. I have matched these key principles with quotes and photographs, assembling them into this book for you. It is a compilation of wisdom and guidance to inspire self-reflection and inner strength. My purpose in writing this book is to share them with you.

I was able to apply my expertise as a former professor of social work on topics of personal resilience, a positive attitude, and effective social problem-solving. As a self-employed actor, writer, and producer, the principles in this book have helped me to stay focused and determined to live my best life.

As my mother used to say, "Keeping a humble perspective is essential, and nothing should be taken for granted." Every morning when I wake up, I feel gratitude for all my blessings and thank God for the new day. Having an optimistic attitude keeps me afloat in stormy weather and unlocks solutions to life's challenges. Having the courage to seize my own power and take responsibility for my own choices has been essential to me, especially as a self-directed entrepreneur.

In the ebb and flow of life's ups and downs, sometimes we must navigate through rough waters en route to safe harbor. When I find myself feeling stressed, strength and renewal are within reach by the ocean. Amid the simple multisensory rhythms of nature—including sounds of ocean waves and seagulls, the smell of salty air and seaweed, and the textures of soft sand and bumpy rocks—I can quiet my mind and self-reflect.

Self-reflection is the key to maintaining a character of integrity, honesty, and responsibility—traits my family has deeply instilled in me. "Always put your best foot forward, Harry," my mother used to say. This advice guided me in business and personal relationships, and helped me keep high expectations of myself. This quote stayed with me since childhood, and I was able to use it not only in working toward a career, but also in relationships. Following this guidance has opened up so many opportunities for me. A strong work ethic pays off.

Doing the right thing often requires being honest with oneself and having the courage to acknowledge one's own emotions. I found that I need to have a realistic and healthy perspective in order to move successfully through life. Sound decisions are made after taking time to cool down when necessary and think rationally before solving problems. As I find my calm, I can feel grounded and develop determination to overcome obstacles.

The voice of reason deep in my gut is my internal compass. It is easier to hear that voice amid the perpetual sound of ocean waves. Despite the weather, the water is like a mirror that registers in my mind a reflection of my true self, where my strengths and flaws become clear. Clarity of thought is a gift of the seaside that helps me find direction and make tough life decisions. I revisit and renew my focus on the real purpose of life, and contemplate whether my present master plan is achievable. Sometimes it is necessary to change direction in order to achieve my true purpose.

Personal growth often requires the courage to step out of the comfort zone. Problems cannot be solved until they are acknowledged and discussed. Tuning in to one's true purpose requires being open and authentic. In reflecting on my mindset, attitude, and knowledge base, I can acknowledge areas to strengthen in order to reach for new horizons. Creative and effective solutions to life's challenges come to mind as I stand in the sand, looking out at the ocean.

No man is an island, so we must always nurture social connections and form bonds of friendship. I recognize that my choices impact those around me and vice versa. We can achieve more together. Socialization is food for my soul. Self-care is also essential. Lasting relationships are built by having honest conversations about things that matter deeply. I found that unlocking the heart requires being open, vulnerable, and flexible in supporting each other. This is how I charted the course in my life and found true peace within.

I hope that the following quotes and pictures will inspire you to live a purposeful life that is full of joy and happiness. As you focus on the serenity, majesty, and beauty of the local seaside, may you, too, find the inner peace, renewed energy, and clarity to experience life fully. May your days be graced with health, hope, and peace as you move safely through uncharted waters on a meaningful and memorable journey to the destinations of your choice.

As my mother used to say, "Tomorrow is not promised." As sure as the sun will rise, each new day brings possibilities for peace, creativity, self-expression, and joy. Embrace them fully. Stay humble, and may wisdom guide you on your journey.

CHAPTER 1

Keeping a Humble Perspective

When you grow up by the sea, you spend a good deal of time looking at the horizon. You wonder what on Earth the waves might bring—and where the sea might deposit you—until one day you know you have lived between two places, the scene of arrival and the point of departure.

—Andrew O'Hagan

The happiest people don't have the best of everything.
They make the best of everything.

—Unknown

Tomorrow is not promised.

—Mildred Thomas

Faith is my sword.
Truth is my shield.
Knowledge my armor.

—Dr. Stephen Strange

Soul, a moving river.
Body, the riverbed.

—Rumi

Dear Ocean,
Thank you for making us feel tiny,
humble, inspired,
and salty all at once.

—Unknown

And I shall watch the ferry boats, and they'll get high,
on a bluer ocean against tomorrow's sky. And I will
never grow so old again, and I will walk and talk,
in gardens all wet with rain.

—Van Morrison

There's nothing wrong with enjoying
looking at the surface of the ocean itself,
except that when you finally see
what goes on underwater,
you realize that you've been missing
the whole point of the ocean.

—Dave Barry

Write your worries in the sand.
Carve your blessings in stone.

—Unknown

CHAPTER 2

Being Grateful

There's never one sunrise the same
or one sunset the same.

—Carlos Santana

If it weren't for the rocks in its bed,
the stream would have no song.

—Carl Perkins

If you change the way you look at things,
the things you look at change.

—Dr. Wayne Dyer

Be grateful that certain things didn't work out.
Sometimes you don't even know what you've been
protected from or where you're being guided to when
you're in the midst of it all. That's why you just have to
trust that greater things are aligning for you.
Let go gracefully.

—Idillionaire

The grass may be greener on the other side of the fence,
but you still have to mow it.

—Anonymous

Don't be a hard rock when you really are a gem.

—Lauryn Hill

Your mind is a ship; it can sail across the universe as long as you don't allow negative thoughts to sink it.

—Matshona Dhliwayo

Summer should get a speeding ticket.

—Anonymous

Sometimes you will never know the true value
of a moment until it becomes a memory.

—Dr. Seuss

CHAPTER 3

Seizing Your Own Power

You were born to stand out. Stop trying to fit in.

—Roy T. Bennett

Go after dreams, not people.

—Paulo Coelho

You are a work of art.
Not everyone will understand you,
but the ones who do
will never forget about you.

—Steven Morrissey

You can either see yourself as a wave in the ocean,
or you can see yourself as the ocean.

—Oprah Winfrey

There is a fountain of youth: it is your mind, your talents, the creativity you bring to your life and the lives of people you love. When you learn to tap this source, you will truly have defeated age.

—Sophia Loren

You've got to be one that, wherever you are, like a flower, you've got to blossom where you're planted. You cannot eliminate darkness. You cannot banish it by cursing darkness. The only way to get rid of darkness is light and to be the light yourself.

—Cory Booker

We are not given a good life or a bad life.
We are given a life,
and it's up to us to make it good or bad.

—Devika Fernando

There are three types of people:
those who make things happen,
those who watch things happen,
and those who wonder what happened.

—Nicholas Murray Butler

O, let my land be a land where Liberty
Is crowned with no false patriotic wreath,
But opportunity is real and life is free,
Equality is in the air we breathe.

—Langston Hughes

CHAPTER 4

Self-Reflecting

Until you cross the bridge of your insecurities,
you can't begin to explore your possibilities.

—Tim Fargo

Life is 10 percent what happens to you
and 90 percent how you react to it.

—Charles R. Swindoll

You can't change what's going on around you until you start changing what's going on within you.

—Zig Ziglar

What can you learn from a statue?
You can learn to stay calm, whatever happens!

—Mehmet Murat İldan

Men do not mirror themselves in running water—
they mirror themselves in still water.
Only what is still can still the stillness of other things.

—Zhuangzi

On the still calm waters of surrender,
the reflections of clarity appear.

—Bryant McGill

Sometimes people don't want to hear the truth
because they don't want their illusions destroyed.

—Friedrich Nietzsche

True power is sitting back and observing things with logic. True power is restraint. If words can control you, that means everyone else can control you. Breathe and allow things to pass.

—Warren Buffett

The past is a place of reference, not a place of residence;
the past is a place of learning, not a place of living.

—Roy T. Bennett

CHAPTER 5

Stepping Out of Your Comfort Zone

Inhale courage, exhale fear.

—Steve Gilliland

Like wildflowers, you must allow yourself to grow in all the places people thought you never would.

—Lorde

Be the change you wish to see in the world.

—Mahatma Gandhi

Don't sit on the fence; break it and move out!
Don't be confined to the little things you do; the sky should be below your limit!

—Israelmore Ayivor

A rock pile ceases to be a rock pile
the moment a single man contemplates it,
bearing within him the image of a cathedral.

—Antoine de Saint-Exupéry

I liked challenging people and making them uncomfortable. That's what leads to introspection and that's what leads to improvement. You could say I dared people to be their best selves.

—Kobe Bryant

Always remember you are braver than you believe,
stronger than you seem,
smarter than you think,
and loved by more than you know.

—A. A. Milne

Never forget that only dead fish swim with the stream.

—Malcolm Muggeridge

May your dreams be larger than mountains and may you have the courage to scale their summits.

—Harley King

CHAPTER 6

Finding Direction and Purpose

The meaning of life is to find your gift.
The purpose of life is to give it away.

—Pablo Picasso

Like the waves in the ocean,
life changes every moment.

—Debasish Mridha

It is better to take many small steps
in the right direction
than to make a great leap forward
only to stumble backward.

—Louis Sachar

Slow down and enjoy life.
It's not only the scenery you miss by going too fast—
you also miss the sense of
where you are going and why.

—Eddie Cantor

Calm sailing doesn't come from calm waters;
it comes from having a good navigator,
a good crew, and a good vessel.

—Anthony T. Hincks

Everything in life happens for a reason.
The challenge in life is to find that reason.

—Empire

If you make the mistake of looking back too much,
you aren't focused enough on the road in front of you.

—Brad Paisley

Sometimes it's a journey that teaches you
a lot about your destination.

—Drake

Change will not come if we wait
for some other person or some other time.
We are the ones we've been waiting for.
We are the change that we seek.

—Barack Obama

CHAPTER 7

Keeping a Strong Work Ethic

The future is worth it.
All the pain.
All the tears.
The future is worth the fight.

—Martian Manhunter

Many people spend too much time trying
to be the captain of someone else's boat.
Learn to be a lighthouse
and the boats will find their way.

—Thomas S. Monson

Change your energy
and you will change your life.

—Roxana Jones

The secret to walkin' on water
is knowing where the rocks are.

—William "Bootsy" Collins

I learned that you don't get anywhere by sitting comfortably in a chair.

—Conrad Hilton

Once you understand
that no one owes you anything,
life becomes much easier.

—Unknown

There is no elevator to success.
You have to take the stairs.

—Zig Ziglar

Without a solid foundation,
you'll have trouble creating anything of value.

—Erika Oppenheimer

CHAPTER 8

Overcoming Obstacles

The sooner you can find the courage
to accept your adversity,
the sooner you can pave a positive path
in your precious life.

—Juri Love

Where flowers bloom,
so does hope.

—Lady Bird Johnson

Rocks in my path?
I keep them all.
With them I shall build my castle.

—Nemo Nox

Knowledge and imagination are the life buoy
and the extra lung for breathing
outside the walls of a tainted reality.

—Hassan Blasim

Flow around obstacles
just like water
flows around rocks.

—Jana Kingsford

If the road to your dreams
is full of potholes,
take the highway.

—Matshona Dhliwayo

Often when someone criticizes you for your choices,
they're really saying
they're unhappy with their own.

—Wendy Williams

Take the stones people throw at you
and use them to build a monument.

—Robin Sharma

Don't be caught up the creek without a paddle.

—Unknown

In the world of chaos,
the old tree stands all alone.

—Srestha Das Choudhury

CHAPTER 9

Making Tough Decisions

The ultimate measure of a man is not
where he stands in moments of
convenience and comfort, but where he stands
at times of challenge and controversy.

—Martin Luther King Jr.

*The hardest thing in life is to know
which bridge to cross and which to burn.*

—David Russell

When you get on the boat that's saving you,
don't pull up the ladder behind you.

—Adrienne Clarkson

Don't waste a minute not being happy.
If one window closes, run to the next window—
or break down a door.

—Brooke Shields

The universe works in crazy ways.
Your good luck will come in waves,
and so does your bad,
so you have to take the good with the bad
and press forward.

—Nick Cummins

When one door closes, another opens;
but we often look so long and so regretfully
upon the closed door
that we do not see the one which has opened for us.

—Alexander Graham Bell

You never really know what's coming.
A small wave, or maybe a big one.
All you can really do is hope that when it comes,
you can surf over it,
instead of drown in its monstrosity.

—Alysha Speer

Sometimes you just have to draw a line in the sand and say, "Enough is enough."

—Harry L. Thomas

All know the way, but few actually walk it.

—Bodhidharma

CHAPTER 10

Nurturing Social Connections

Don't forget that maybe you are
the lighthouse in someone's storm.

—Unknown

We'd be trying to touch the sky
from the bottom of the ocean.
I realize that if we boosted one another,
maybe we'd get a little closer.

—Ruta Sepetys

We are all in this together.
Like a guardian angel, the lighthouse stands,
sending out hope in the night.
Like a faithful friend reaching out a hand
bringing comfort, truth, and light.

—Unknown

We may have all come on different ships,
but we're in the same boat now.

—Martin Luther King Jr.

In a world where you can be anything, be kind.

—Unknown

Build a bridge by extending your hand.

—Ken Poirot

Be careful what you will tolerate.
You are teaching people how to treat you.

—Unknown

Be somebody who makes everybody
feel like a somebody.

—Montague Workshop

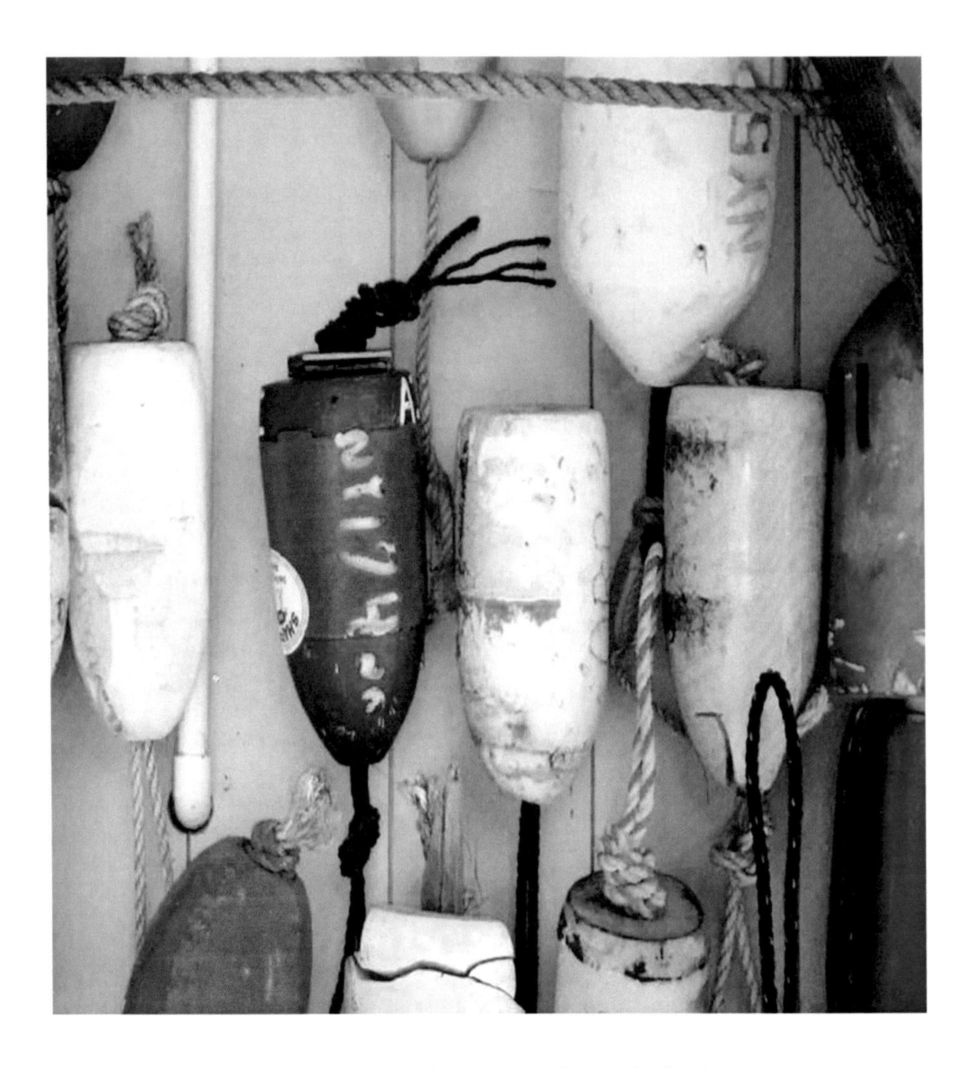

It's always helpful to have somebody help buoy you in difficult times and problem-solve with and to share the marvelous moments with, as well.

—Jane Poynter

CHAPTER 11

Unlocking the Heart

Two empty chairs are not a good use of space.
Fill them up with love.

—Jarod Kintz

A flower cannot blossom without sunshine,
and man cannot live without love.

—Max Müller

Live every moment,
laugh every day,
love beyond words.

—Unknown

"It's impossible," said pride.
"It's risky," said experience.
"It's pointless," said reason.
"Give it a try," whispered the heart.

—Unknown

It is the nature of the strong heart,
that like the palm tree
it strives ever upwards when it is most burdened.

—Sir Philip Sidney

Is it important to have a relationship
written in the stars
or written in the sand?

—Harry L. Thomas

Solitude is not the same as loneliness.
Solitude is a solitary boat
floating in a sea of possible companions.

—Robert Fulghum

The biggest lesson I've learned this year
is to not force anything;
conversations, friendships, relationships, attention, love.
Anything forced is just not worth fighting for.
Whatever flows, flows. Whatever crashes, crashes.
It is what it is.

—Miss Kitty's Random Thoughts on Love, Life and Laughter

Love is like breathing.
You take it in and let it out.

—Wally Lamb

CHAPTER 12

Finding Peace Within

The time to relax is when you don't have time for it.

—Sydney J. Harris

Clouds do not really look like camels
or sailing ships or castles in the sky.
They are simply a natural process at work.
So too, perhaps, are our lives.

—Roger Ebert

The problems of today will soon be buried by the sand of time.

—Unknown

Sky above,
sand below,
peace within.

—Unknown

At the beach, life is different.
Time doesn't move from hour to hour,
but mood to moment.
We live by the currents,
plan by the tides, and follow the sun.

—Sandy Gingras

Be like a fresh flowing stream.

—Lailah Gifty Akita

To escape and sit quietly on the beach—
that's my idea of paradise.

—Emilia Wickstead

You've been given one opportunity
at this thing called life,
so live each day as if it might be your last.
One life. Live it!

—Pastor Sean Smith

Everything you want in life is coming.
So, relax and let the universe pick the timing.

—Unknown

THIS IS YOUR LIFE.
DO WHAT YOU LOVE,
AND DO IT OFTEN.
IF YOU DON'T LIKE SOMETHING, CHANGE IT.
IF YOU DON'T LIKE YOUR JOB, QUIT.
IF YOU DON'T HAVE ENOUGH TIME, STOP WATCHING TV.
IF YOU ARE LOOKING FOR THE LOVE OF YOUR LIFE, STOP;
THEY WILL BE WAITING FOR YOU WHEN YOU
START DOING THINGS YOU LOVE.
STOP OVER ANALYZING,
LIFE IS SIMPLE.
ALL EMOTIONS ARE BEAUTIFUL.
WHEN YOU EAT, APPRECIATE
EVERY LAST BITE.
OPEN YOUR MIND, ARMS, AND HEART TO NEW THINGS
AND PEOPLE, WE ARE UNITED IN OUR DIFFERENCES.
ASK THE NEXT PERSON YOU SEE WHAT THEIR PASSION IS,
AND SHARE YOUR INSPIRING DREAM WITH THEM.
TRAVEL OFTEN; GETTING LOST WILL
HELP YOU FIND YOURSELF.
SOME OPPORTUNITIES ONLY COME ONCE, SEIZE THEM.
LIFE IS ABOUT THE PEOPLE YOU MEET, AND
THE THINGS YOU CREATE WITH THEM
SO GO OUT AND START CREATING.
LIFE IS SHORT.
LIVE YOUR DREAM
AND SHARE
YOUR PASSION.

Peace by the Sea Mindfulness Exercises

Laurie Heyden, MS

The visual image of the sea is a powerful source of peace. You can use the visual image of the sea to your advantage at any time. You don't have to actually be near the water; you can visit the sea in a photograph or visualize it in your mind.

Below are two strategies you can use separately—or, more powerfully, together—to find inner peace. The "Take a Vacation" Strategy and the "Listen to Your Breathing" Strategy can be used together for maximum serenity.

The "Take a Vacation" Strategy

The "Take a Vacation" Strategy is a powerful tool for self-renewal. It requires no travel and can be used at any time. Revisit Harry's peaceful photographic image at any time—in the book or in your imagination. Choose your favorite peaceful photograph or an image of a peaceful place you are familiar with or may have visited. Picture it in your mind. You can close your eyes and imagine you are there in the scene. The brain is tricked to believe that whatever visual image we put in our own mind is real. We can use this interesting phenomenon to our advantage. The human body reacts to the images we put in our minds.

For example, if you think of terrifying images, your body may react with tense muscles and an elevated heartbeat. If you think of peaceful images, your breathing will become slower and your muscles will relax. If you think of a beach on a warm day, you may feel your muscles relax from the warmth of the sun.

Put beautiful pictures in your mind. Take a vacation in your mind anytime you need to, even if only for a minute. The longer you focus on your peaceful image in your mind, the more peaceful you will feel.

Try it. Enjoy it as often as you need to. It is a good coping skill to add to your toolbox.

The "Listen to Your Breathing" Strategy

The "Listen to Your Breathing" Strategy is a very simple and powerful way to find peace. It is very easy to do. You basically do nothing, but just breathe normally and focus on it. Listening to our own breathing helps us become centered, calm, and focused. It changes our energy level to a more peaceful one. We become calm, focused, and ready for our next task in life. It starts working in as little as fifteen seconds, but the longer you do it, the better it works. I recommend doing this for several minutes.

It is a good activity to do at passive times, like while resting in bed, waiting in line, or riding in a car. Remember, for maximum serenity, close your eyes and visualize a peaceful seaside scene while you listen to your breathing.

Meditation for Peace

Let's get started.

Listen to your breathing. Notice the breath that gives you life. Just breathe regularly, not deeply. Notice the inhales and the exhales. Remember, don't take deep breaths in this exercise. Just breathe normally. Notice the inhales and the exhales that continue on effortlessly within you. Notice the miracle of your breath, the miracle of your life. Be grateful for this miracle that keeps you alive. Let the oxygen-rich air fill your lungs, fortify your body, and nourish your mind.

Continue listening to your breathing until you become so quiet that you notice the beating of your heart deep within you. Focus on your heartbeat now. Notice its location in your chest. Notice the sensation in your chest. Notice your heartbeat's strength and its gentleness. Notice that you are perfectly unique and completely alive. Embrace the possibility of self-love, and feel renewed. Feel the peace that surrounds you. Inhale the peace that you deserve, the peace that you need, the peace that makes you whole.

Be thankful for the gift of you to the universe. Be grateful to the universe for the breath in your lungs, the beating of your heart, and the purpose for your hands. You are beautifully formed. Your heart has so much love to give.

Open your heart to the possibility of acting purely out of kindness. Feel the courage in your heart. It was always there. You have everything you need within you. You are perfectly made, unique, and irreplaceable. You are a special and beautiful creation so worthy of love. You are worthy to give love and worthy to receive love.

Let love surround you. Welcome love into all of your steps and all of your paths. Have faith that you will recognize the purpose to which you are called. Trust that you will see the connections in your life that need to be made stronger.

With every inhale, take in hope. Your breath gives life, hope, and possibility. When you take the time to listen to your own breathing and notice your own heartbeat, you will find within you the ability to quiet your soul and discern the purpose for your life. You already know the right thing to do. Trust in your ability to choose, embrace, and live your purpose.

Focus again on your breath.

Inhale strength. Exhale weakness. Inhale courage. Exhale insecurity.

Inhale wisdom. Exhale doubt. Inhale love. Exhale loneliness.

Speak strength into your heart. "I am strong. I am brave. I am smart. I am wise. I am capable. I am enough. I am worthy of love. I got this."

Now, look and see the beauty and possibilities of this day.

About the Author

Harry L. Thomas, MSW, is an active humanitarian who enjoys helping people get on the right track to live their best lives. He earned his master's degree from the University of Connecticut's School of Social Work. As an adjunct professor, he presented engaging lectures at Eastern Connecticut State University. He lives for lively conversations on what really matters to people. His friends look forward to his daily social-media posts of his personal photography carefully matched with uplifting quotes.

Harry is also an actor, writer, and producer. Recently, he has written and produced commercials and public-service announcements dealing with current social issues, such as social justice, mental health, and personal well-being. He thrives on inspiring change through careful combinations of images and words. Harry commonly appears as an actor in television shows, movies, and commercials. He is proud to be a member of the Screen Actors Guild – American Federation of Television and Radio Artists (SAG-AFTRA). He has appeared with Hollywood actors including Al Pacino, Kevin Costner, Adam Sandler, and others. Due to his deep love of music, he also enjoys the art of freelancing as a video DJ. He is a member of the Chamber of Commerce of Eastern Connecticut and the Greater Norwich Chamber of Commerce.

Photography has captivated Harry ever since receiving his first camera as a child. Capturing appealing moments and visual images on film has always been a passion. He has earned local recognition and awards for his photography throughout his life.

Harry grew up in New London, Connecticut, in a family of professional actors and models. His mother, a professional model, got him involved in the business at age five, appearing in commercials.

He enjoys traveling to tropical destinations, especially Hawaii, Bermuda, and the Caribbean. His favorite pastimes are dancing and collecting vintage vinyl records. Harry resides in New London's shoreline community.

Email: scriptproducerHLT@gmail.com

Facebook: @peacebytheseaharrythomas

Twitter: @Thomas_Actor

Instagram: actor_ht

Vimeo: Harry Thomas Actor-Producer

About the Editor

Laurie Heyden, MS, is a school psychologist and artist from Warren, Rhode Island. She enjoys teaching coping skills and empowering students to have the courage to be leaders by doing the right thing. She believes that social problem-solving skills are as important to success as reading, writing, and math. She has special interests in prevention and brain-based learning. Her personal mission is to be a catalyst for positive change by empowering others to find, develop, and use their gifts so that they can live happier and more fulfilling lives. She cofounded the Bristol Kindness Project, a grassroots effort to spread hope and love in the local community. Her hobbies include ballroom dancing, painting kindness rocks, and designing jewelry with beads from around the world.

Email: laheyden@hotmail.com